This book is to be returned on or before
the last date stamped below.

THE
MOSAIC
SOURCEBOOK

THE
MOSAIC
SOURCEBOOK

Projects ▪ Designs ▪ Motifs

Paul Siggins & Paul Cooper

▪

Text by Jenna Jarman

Photography by Richard Foster

CONRAN
OCTOPUS

For Fiona, Phoebe, Jess and Carol.
Thanks for the support.

First published in 1997 by
Conran Octopus Limited
37 Shelton Street
London WC2H 9HN

Editorial Director: Suzannah Gough
Senior Editor: Jenna Jarman
Editorial Assistant: Helen Woodhall

Designer: Amanda Lerwill
Stylist: Tiffany Davis
Art Direction: Sue Storey assisted
                         by Amanda Lerwill

Production: Mano Mylvaganam

British Library Cataloguing-in-Publication Data
A catalogue record for this book is available from
the British Library.

ISBN 1 85029 915 3

Printed in Singapore by KHL Printing Co. Pte. Ltd

CONTENTS

Foreword

As contemporary mosaicists who like to have freedom with design, we take our inspiration from a wide range of sources, from classical mosaic art to contemporary culture. Our approach is characteristically simple and understated, but we enjoy working in a variety of styles and often incorporate bold colours and motifs into our designs.

Our view on materials is that there should be as few restrictions as possible – if it doesn't perish then you can mosaic with it. In addition to traditional tesserae, we also use glass beads, buttons, pebbles and shells amongst other things, and have a large collection of ceramic tiles, gathered from years of rummaging round flea markets, car boot sales and tile suppliers' discontinued shelves. With these materials we produce all sorts of mosaic pieces – decorative objects, wall hangings, floor panels, as well as more unusual three-dimensional forms, such as mannequins, busts and clocks.

Although mosaic is a relatively simple and certainly accessible craft, it can seem daunting to the uninitiated. In this book we aim to give all the information a beginner needs to get started, and also to provide the more experienced with a rich source of innovative designs and motifs. For us, mosaic is a highly rewarding and therapeutic craft, and we hope that everyone will share in our enjoyment of it, both as an art form and as an outlet for self-expression.

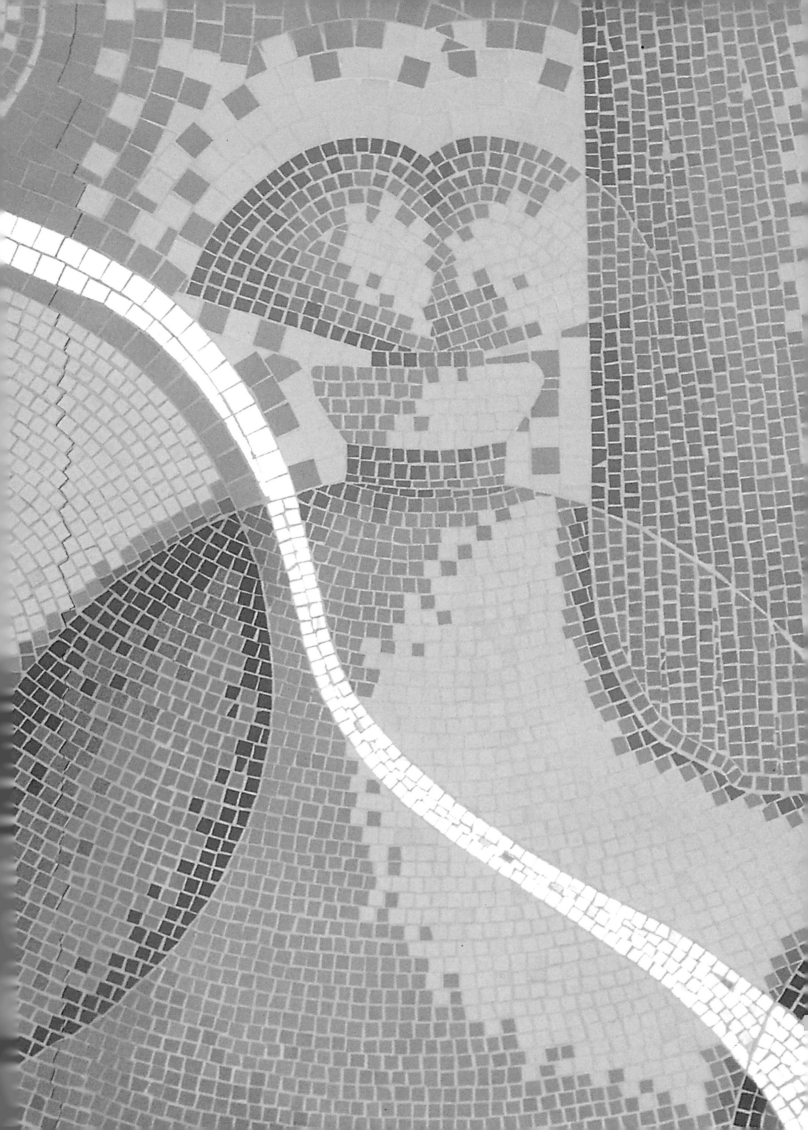

Introduction

The ancient art of mosaic is enjoying a new and exciting surge of popularity, both as a craft and as a consumer item. No longer is mosaic associated only with classical and religious works of art, or the gaudier designs of the Seventies; today mosaic is a highly flexible medium at the cutting edge of design, and there are striking mosaic borders, panels and murals decorating homes, restaurants, bars and offices everywhere. Capable of taking on many guises, mosaic can be simply defined as a pattern or image made up of small pieces of material, called tesserae, which covers a surface. The possibilities are endless in terms of designs, materials and uses – for both decorative objects and architectural features – and more and more people are realizing how rewarding yet accessible mosaic is as a craft or hobby.

Mosaic was of course hugely popular during classical antiquity and the Middle Ages, and both periods produced many great works of art. It was, however, reserved only for those wealthy enough to commission what was a very expensive medium: during the Middle Ages, for example, mosaic was almost exclusively the preserve of the Church. Its role was to some extent a subservient one to that of painting – Roman and Hellenistic works were created chiefly as durable copies after paintings; and

medieval mosaicists, although appreciating mosaic's special luminous qualities, strove to bring their art as close to that of painting as possible. This confusion between the two disciplines helped lead to the decline of mosaic during the

The sea was the source of inspiration for the design of this mirror frame, decorated in complementary shades of blue vitreous glass tesserae. It was an experimental piece made while we were developing our two-dimensional relief frames.

Renaissance, and it is only relatively recently that mosaic has been re-evaluated, and that the means of production have brought mosaic within the reach of ordinary people.

It was during the last century that attitudes towards mosaic began to change. Not only did it start to be put on an industrial and commercial basis, but certain artists also began to question its role and revitalize it as an art form. The innovative use of materials by Catalan artist and architect Antonio Gaudí (1852–1926), for example, was key in modernizing mosaic style. By mixing materials and techniques in contemporary, non-representational designs, Gaudí was particularly influential; his wild and wonderful, largely exterior mosaics, made up of smalti, bits of glass bottles, crockery and ceramic, showed how large surfaces could be decorated with cheap, alternative materials. Form and style were revitalized and the way was now open for mosaic to expand.

In the middle of this century, the mass production of vitreous glass tesserae brought material costs down and so broadened the appeal of mosaic. This significant step forward had its

disadvantages, however, as it led to a plethora of uninspired mosaics from the Fifties onwards – a trend which reached its nadir in the Seventies when, for many, mosaic was almost synonymous with the decoration of swimming pools. Fortunately, individual artists continued to make innovative and interesting mosaics during this period and now mainstream mosaic is not only within everyone's reach, but it is also recognized as an exciting and stylish medium in its own right.

You can use an endless variety of materials to create mosaics. For this one we used glass beads, broken ceramics, cut tesserae and a reclaimed art deco border on a base of medium-density fibreboard (MDF). The wrought-iron frame was specially made but you could use a ready-made one.

varying angles to catch the light, for example, and the interstices or spacing between the tesserae can either be widened in order to maximize stylization, or else tightly packed for a more painterly effect.

Making mosaics is not only easy but can also be immensely satisfying and therapeutic. As with a jigsaw or collage, this craft has an almost childlike appeal as the tesserae are carefully pieced together to form a whole. Perhaps the most appealing thing about mosaic, however, is the huge flexibility it offers, in terms of individual choices of materials and textures, as well as designs, styles and uses. Mosaics can be made to fit any style of interior whether traditional or contemporary. Most of the projects in this book are particularly well suited to contemporary interiors, but they still incorporate classical and traditional designs, and with the broad mix of colour schemes and motifs on offer, there are styles to suit all tastes.

Everything depends on the mix of colours and materials and, as this book demonstrates, a mosaic

Although capable of producing stunning results, mosaic does not necessarily demand artistic flair nor even good drawing skills. The stylized quality of mosaic means that even the simplest designs can be strikingly effective, and there is a wealth of source material available both in this book and elsewhere – from classic to contemporary designs – for you to refer to or copy. And the original design is just the beginning – tesserae can be set at

ABOVE LEFT: *This table is made of carved plywood, and the snake is made from cement resin. The tesserae are all one colour so that the snake blends in with the rest of the mosaic, as it does with its environment in nature.*

ABOVE: *The use of smalti gives this asp vessel a timeless appearance – the aim was to create the kind of mosaic which could have adorned an ancient temple, perhaps concealing mysterious and dark secrets.*

Small or portable objects are obviously a good starting point for the beginner. And as mosaic covers a multitude of sins, such as dull colours or hideous patterns, even old or ugly items can be transformed completely. But tackling larger surfaces doesn't have to be daunting, although this will obviously take longer; and time can be saved if mosaic pieces or panels are mixed in with plain areas (see pages 22–3). And as little in the way of tools and equipment is needed, anybody can start making mosaics with the minimum amount of investment. So, whatever your needs and whatever your style, mosaic has something to offer you. This book will get beginners started on this fascinating craft and will inspire the more experienced, enabling everyone to make stunning mosaics for friends and the home.

can be as vibrantly patterned or as subtle and understated as needed. The possibilities for both colours and materials are endless: commercially produced tesserae offer an infinite spectrum of colours and an interesting range of textures, from shiny glass to smooth porcelain, gloss or matt ceramic; and grouting can be any colour you wish. Then there are all the more unusual materials to consider, such as pebbles, shells and beads, to name just a few.

But the choices don't end there. Mosaic can be used not only to cover floors and walls, but also to decorate furniture and other objects around the home.

ABOVE: *On one side of this urn blazing reds and golds reflect the vibrancy of the sun; on the other, softer colours depict the moon.*

ABOVE RIGHT: *The extravagant use of silver leaf mosaic on this large mirror frame is complemented by the simplicity of the scrolled form. To keep costs down, silver leaf can be combined with other materials, such as porcelain tesserae, as in the silver star picture frame project on page 38.*

How to use this book

The following notes explain what each section of the book is about and how it should be used, either by the complete beginner or the more experienced craftsperson.

TECHNIQUES, TOOLS AND MATERIALS

Techniques (pages 14–23). Despite potentially stunning results, the technique for mosaic is surprisingly simple – easily explained and learnt, and little changed since ancient times. It involves cutting material into basic shapes, pasting them into place according to a pattern, and then finally setting the mosaic with grout. In this section, the two techniques for doing this – the direct and indirect methods – are both clearly explained with comprehensive step-by-step photography for two easy projects. The key differences between the two methods, and their advantages and disadvantages, are outlined so that you can feel confident about deciding which method to use. All the projects in the book are based on one or other of these techniques, to which you can always refer if necessary.

Tools and materials (pages 16–19). A comprehensive list of the basic equipment, accompanied by photographs, is given (see pages 16–17), with items then described in detail. Few specialist tools are needed for mosaic – the tile cutter and nipper (a tool for cutting fairly precise and small shapes) are the only essential ones and both are inexpensive and easy to find. Other tools, such as sponges and squeegees, are found in most homes. The possibilities for materials are endless, from commercially available tesserae and tiles (vitreous glass, smalti and ceramic), to everyday materials (pebbles, smashed crockery, beads and shells). This section describes the options, providing information on potential uses, availability, cost, advantages and disadvantages.

PROJECTS

The eight step-by-step projects can all be made within the space of a weekend, and all by the beginner. Some, however, are better suited than others to the complete novice, and this is indicated in the introductions. Throughout the look is clean and contemporary, and the projects provide an exciting range of innovative styles and colourways – from a vibrant African-style tabletop to a classically inspired and understated lampbase. With these you will be able to create all the most popular mosaic pieces that command such high prices in today's best furnishing stores, including picture and mirror frames, garden urns, vases and decorative dishes – mosaics both for outdoors and for a range of interiors.

The projects use an interesting variety of materials, and colour codes are provided for commercially available tesserae so that you can reproduce the projects exactly if you wish. Templates and alternative designs for the projects are also provided (see Alternative Designs, right).

This 6m (20ft) long panel was commissioned for the perfumery and cosmetics department of Dickins and Jones in London. The porcelain tesserae of the bottle shapes are cut through with ribbons of gold and silver which seem to move as they catch the light.

ALTERNATIVE DESIGNS

For each project there are two alternative designs provided, using different colour schemes, sometimes in a similar style and sometimes giving a completely different look. The kitsch floral vase project, for example, comes with two distinctive alternative designs – one combining pieces of smashed blue-and-white crockery with pale shells to create an unusually delicate effect, the other a lively and abstract pattern incorporating a random mix of red and purple beads. Any of these designs could be adapted to your own colour schemes, or applied to other objects, and would work particularly well on similarly shaped ones such as lampbases, urns and pots of any kind. Once again, the idea is to provide maximum flexibility, while the basic technique illustrated in the step-by-step photography can still be followed. Whilst still suitable for the beginner – though the complete novice may be advised to try one of the step-by-step projects before experimenting with alternatives – these sixteen alternative designs provide a wealth of original source material to inspire even the most accomplished mosaicist.

TEMPLATES AND MOTIFS

Project templates (pages 78–85). Each project is accompanied by a template so that the design can be clearly seen and easily followed. These can be photocopied, enlarged and transferred onto your surface, copied freehand or used simply as a guideline. You can obviously choose the extent to which you stick to the design – the templates are not prescriptive but are simply there for those who feel they need or want them. You could easily adapt the design, change the colour scheme, or use the basic template for whatever object you choose (a template for a tabletop, for example, could just as well be used for a dish or plate). None of the designs are overly complicated, though some are obviously simpler than others.

Miscellaneous motifs (pages 86–95). This ten-page section of motifs provides further source material for those looking for new ideas and inspiration. The motifs can be used in a variety of ways: a single motif could be used on a plain background; it could be incorporated into one of the designs provided in the book; multiple motifs could be dotted randomly over a plain surface, or placed deliberately to form a border or central pattern. The possibilities are endless, and, as with the design templates in the book, they can be photocopied, traced, or copied freehand. The motifs are shaded so that you can get the right effect using the colour scheme of your choice, and the basic methods used are the same as those outlined in the techniques section.

Organized in different categories, the motifs range from the representational (flowers, fish, shells) to the abstract or geometric (for all-over patterns or borders), and offer classical, ethnic, Celtic, art deco and contemporary styles.

TECHNIQUES

Tools & materials

1. Grout float
2. Block of wood
3. Combed scraper
4. Small pointing trowel
5. Straight scraper
6. Serrated trowel
7. Ready-mixed tile adhesive
8. White grout
9. Spray oil
10 & 11. Poster paint
12. Nippers
13. Hammer
14. Plastic tile cutter and breaker
15. Glass cutter
16. Metal tile cutter and breaker
17. Brown paper
18. Scissors
19. Craft knife
20. Water-soluble pen
21. Pencil
22. Permanent marker
23. Scalpel
24. Artist's brush
25. Brush
26. Dust mask
27. Goggles
28. Steel ruler
29. Cement-based tile adhesive
30. Smalti
31. Ceramic tiles
32. Vitreous glass tesserae
33. Beads
34. Porcelain tesserae
35. PVA washable glue
36. Silver leaf mosaic
37. Pebbles
38. Tea towel
39. Lint-free cloth
40. Sponge

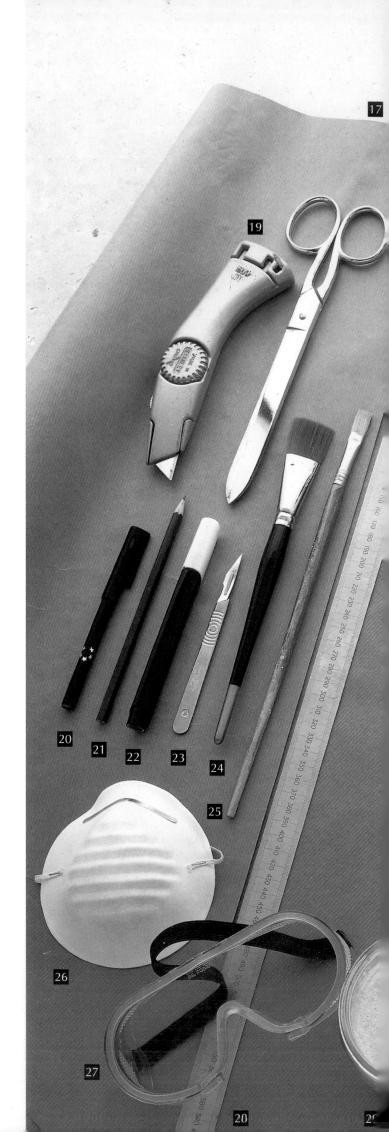

Most of the following tools and materials are available from mosaic and some tile suppliers. For information on suppliers, including mail order, see page 96.

TESSERAE

These are the small pieces of material that are built up onto a surface to form mosaic. Listed below are the most common types, but there are many more to choose from – beads, bottletops, gemstones, scraps of metal (but be careful of rust), as well as stones and pebbles for outdoor mosaics.

Ceramic tiles Household kitchen or bathroom tiles may be plain white or highly coloured or patterned, in matt or gloss finishes. They can be a cheap option – look out for old or reject tiles as even the gaudiest ones have potential once they are cut up into small pieces. Smashed crockery is also suitable for mosaic, as are home-fired and painted ceramics. Ceramic is easy enough to cut with a tile cutter, although perhaps not as easy as vitreous glass. It is not usually frost-proof and so is not suitable for outdoor mosaics.

Porcelain and vitrified clay Hard-wearing materials which can be used for both indoor and outdoor mosaics, these are particularly suitable for floors. Both come in a matt, natural and muted colour range, and will stain easily if not properly sealed. Porcelain is inexpensive (cheaper than vitreous glass) and is sold by the sheet (size and number of tesserae vary). Vitrified clay tends to be thicker and therefore slightly more hard-wearing and expensive, as well as more difficult to cut. It is sold either as tiles or tesserae.

Smalti These are thick, rectangular chunks of opaque glass – approx. 10 x 15 x 7mm (⅜ x ½ x ¼in) – which are uneven and so suitable when a totally flat surface is not required. They come in a vast range of colours, and are glossy and highly reflective – ideal if you want your mosaic to glint and catch the light. Handmade, mainly in Italy, smalti is expensive and sold by the half-kilo. All colours are the same price (with the exception of gold and silver). It is suitable for both indoor and outdoor use but not for heavy-duty flooring.

Vitreous glass tesserae These are also made of opaque glass but are thinner and cheaper than smalti. They are manufactured to regular 2 x 2 x 4mm (¾ x ¾ x 1½in) squares, with a smooth front and rippled back to aid adhesion. They come in a wide range of colours, although not as wide as that of smalti, and prices vary according to the colour. Gold and silver tesserae are the most costly and so are ideal for limited use or highlights. Their thinness and regular shape makes them easy to cut and use, and so they are ideal for the beginner, and can be used when a totally flat surface is required. They are resistant to poor weather conditions and are suitable for outdoor use. Vitreous glass tesserae are sold loose, in single colours or in mixed bags (usually sold by the kilo) or by the sheet (225 tesserae), either in one colour only, or ready mixed into a multi-colour, simple geometric design. Stuck down on paper which you simply peel off, these tesserae can be applied immediately, without any nipping or cutting, if you want to mosaic a surface quickly.

There are a number of brands available, and any can be used for mosaic. We used Vetricolor (also known as Vitmos) for our projects and colour codes for this brand are provided so that you can reproduce our colours exactly if you wish.

TOOLS

Combed scraper Used to give an even and grooved bed of adhesive on flat surfaces.

Glass cutter This simple tool has a tungsten wheel to score straight or curved lines on ceramic, vitreous glass or mirror. Lubricate the wheel by spraying it with oil before use to make its action smoother.

Hammer and hardie These are traditional tools which are sometimes used for cutting marble and smalti. They require practice and so are not used in this book; the tools described here are more suitable for beginners.

Nippers These are mosaic cutters or tile nippers with tungsten tips, used for halving or quartering tesserae, or for 'nibbling' them into precise shapes. They are ideal when working with vitreous glass, ceramic tesserae or smalti, but can be hard work on porcelain or vitrified clay.

Permanent pen For marking designs or guidelines on the surface of objects – water-soluble ink would be rubbed off by adhesive. Do not use on tesserae.

Serrated trowel Used in the same way as a combed scraper but for larger areas, such as walls and floors.

Small pointing trowel Useful for applying adhesive to small, awkward areas.

Squeegees and grout floats These are used for spreading the grout into the joints between tesserae. When using the squeegee, use the blade to drag the grout across; with the grout float, use the edge and not the flat surface.

Straight scraper General adhesive application tool.

Tile cutter and breaker This dual-purpose tool, which comes in either plastic or metal, can both score and cut. The plastic variety have a short life but are extremely cheap, and are suitable for vitreous glass, ceramic and thin porcelain; the metal ones will last longer and can be used to break harder materials, such as thick porcelain and vitrified clay tiles as well as ceramic and glass. With both, the scored line is placed in the centre of the breaker's jaws which, once shut, will break the tile along the line.

Water-soluble pen For marking guidelines on glazed tesserae for cutting. Note that you should never use this or any pen on unglazed tesserae.

GLUES AND ADHESIVES

Cement This is cheap and strong. It can be used on walls and is ideal for laying external mosaic flooring as long as conditions are frost-free.

Cement-based tiling adhesives These powder-mix adhesives provide long-lasting results (but check the label of different brands for drying times as these vary) and are suitable for most tesserae, and all surfaces that need to be hard-wearing, for indoor and outdoor use. When applying to a flexible surface such as board or timber, mix in a flexible additive which will soften the adhesive in case there is any movement in the timber. Rapid-setting powder adhesives (a few hours) are also available.

Grout This is cement mortar which is the commonly used material for setting the finished mosaic. For the projects in this book where there are quite wide gaps between tesserae, a wide-joint grout (which has a sandy texture) is used. If the interstices are small, however, and tesserae are tightly packed together, then grouting is not actually necessary.

It depends on taste: some people prefer the grouted look, and some the ungrouted. Grouting does, however, strengthen the mosaic and give a smoother, less jagged finish. Grouts are available in a range of colours, the basic ones being white, grey, ivory, charcoal, sandstone and brown. Specialist coloured grouts are also available but it is very easy to make these yourself by mixing white grout with poster or powder paint (water-based only). Remember that coloured grouts will be a couple of shades lighter when dry.

PVA adhesive sealer Mixed 1 part to 4 parts water, this is used to seal all sides of untreated wood to prevent swelling when moisture gets in – either during or after the mosaic process. It is also used to seal terracotta and other porous surfaces. Some people use undiluted PVA as an adhesive for sticking down tesserae, but this is not recommended as it is not sufficiently durable. Available from DIY suppliers.

Ready-mixed tile adhesives These are not as hard-wearing as the powder-mix variety but are convenient and can be bought in smaller quantities. They are hard-wearing enough for indoor decorative objects – made of glass, ceramic, wood – but are not recommended for floors. Water-resistant brands are also available and are advisable for mosaics that may get completely wet, or for those on wooden objects, but even the non water-resistant brands are regularly used for bathroom tiling. Products that are a combination of adhesive and grout are not recommended.

Silicone sealants and multi-purpose gap-filling adhesives Both of these are useful for very small tesserae that need to dry quickly, but are not suitable for large areas. They come in tubes or cartridges that fit into a gun which can be used to lay a neat, accurate bead of adhesive along a line. Silicone sealant is slightly more difficult to clean off when dry. These adhesives can be used for glass, plastic, ceramic, metal and wood.

Washable PVA glue Mixed 1 part to 3 parts water, this is used to apply tesserae to brown paper for the indirect method. Available from art shops.

SAFETY NOTE Goggles should be worn when cutting tesserae as small bits of material can fly through the air. A mask should be worn when sawing fibreboard, polishing off dry grout and using solvents. Rubber gloves are advised for all procedures involving cement, grout and acid.

THE DIRECT METHOD

Basic Equipment
Dust mask
Lint-free cloth
Nippers
Pencil and ruler
Pot for mixing grout/PVA/adhesive
Protective glasses
Scraper
Sponge
Squeegee

Tools
Craft knife
2.5cm (1in) artist's brush

Materials
Circular block of MDF 18mm (¾in)
    thick, 23cm (9in) in diameter
PVA sealer (1 part PVA glue to
    4 parts water)
1 litre (1¾pt) pot of ready-mixed
    water-resistant tile adhesive
Vitreous glass tesserae (Vetricolor):
    70 x dark blue (20.46.2)
    25 x light blue (20.87.1)
    40 x white (20.10.1)
1.5kg (3lb) bag of white wide-
    joint grout

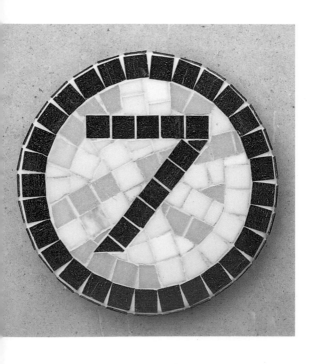

This is a very straightforward method of applying mosaic, in which tesserae are stuck directly onto the chosen object. It is used where the surface does not need to be smooth or completely flat. It is also useful where a large number of colours is being used because the tesserae colours remain visible, whereas in the indirect method – where tesserae are stuck face down – only the backs of the tesserae are seen and these are often not coloured. This method is also used for 3-D work. It is not so suitable for intricate designs, however, as the adhesive applied to the surface will cover and at least partly obscure the design you are following.

A variety of tesserae can be used and combined, including vitreous glass, smalti, mirror, and smashed or broken crockery, as well as more unusual materials such as pebbles, stones and beads. The tesserae can be of varying thicknesses and can be deliberately set at different angles to catch the light.

1 If you are working on a wooden or MDF surface as here, key all over using the craft knife and then prime with PVA sealer, using the artist's brush. Leave to dry.

2 Draw your design on the surface, either freehand, if you feel confident enough, or using a template, basing it on the size of your tesserae. It is also possible to trace designs or use a photocopy of a design.

3 Paste on the adhesive in sections to avoid it drying out and stick down the tesserae (smooth side up), according to the design. In general we advise leaving a 2mm (¹⁄₁₆in) grout gap

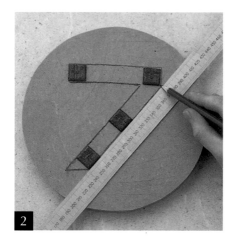

between tesserae, but this depends on the individual project and on personal preference. Here, whole tesserae are stuck down first and the smaller pieces are cut (see step 4) and stuck down as and when necessary. For projects requiring lots of quarter- or half-tesserae, you should cut all of these before starting to paste.

4 To nip the tesserae into smaller pieces – whether wedge shapes, quarters or triangles – hold the nippers on the very edge of the tessera as shown and cut. The whole tessera will then split in a straight line from the point where the nippers are held.

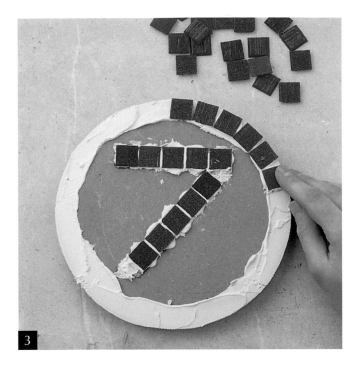

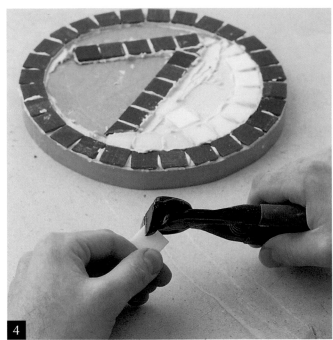

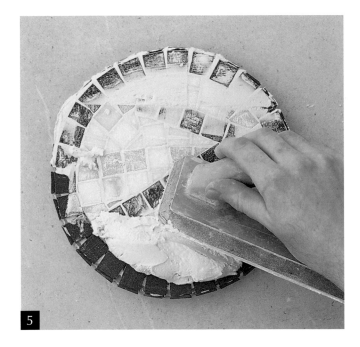

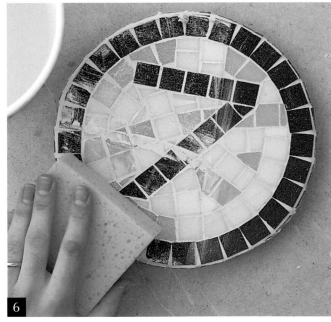

5 Once all the tesserae are stuck down, leave to dry for 24 hours. You will then need to seal the surface of the mosaic by grouting. Gradually mix the grout with water until it is the consistency of a thick creamy paste. Cover the mosaic, including the edge, with a generous amount of grout, using a squeegee or a grout float (or a smaller tool, if necessary, for 3-D work) to ensure that all the gaps and cracks are filled.

6 Wipe off excess grout with the squeegee, and then clean off the residue with a damp sponge.

Once the grout has dried – after approx. 24 hours, polish the mosaic with a clean, dry cloth.

THE INDIRECT METHOD

Basic Equipment (see page 20)

Tools
Permanent marker
Water-soluble pen
Tile cutter and breaker (see page 19)
Tea towel
Hammer
2.5cm (1in) artist's brush
Combed scraper/spatula
Block of wood or grout float
Craft knife

Materials
Brown paper
Ceramic tiles 15cm x 15cm
   (6in x 6in):
   1 x yellow
   1 x blue
   1 x red
Washable PVA glue (1 part PVA
   glue to 3 parts water)
1 litre (1¾pt) pot of ready-mixed
   tile adhesive
1.5kg (3lb) bag of white wide-
   joint grout

This method is ideal for intricate designs which, in the direct method, would be obscured by adhesive. It is used when a very flat, smooth surface is needed. Using this method, the tesserae are first stuck face down onto brown paper with transparent, washable PVA glue before the whole mosaic is transferred onto your chosen object with adhesive.

It is also the best method for large pieces done off-site, as the design can be drawn on paper and cut into segments before the whole thing is transferred to the site and re-assembled like a jigsaw. Other reasons for using this method include: working with multiple pieces (it is easier to do several at a time on paper rather than one at a time with the direct method); working on a horizontal rather than a vertical surface; stopping and starting work on a project (washable PVA glue can be pasted and then pasted again at a later date, whereas in the direct method, the adhesive will harden quickly and will have to be scraped off before re-application is possible).

One of the disadvantages of this method is that when using ceramic tiles, the backs of which are very

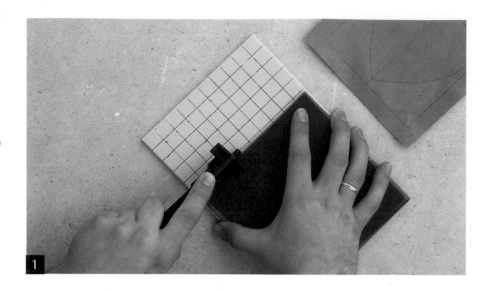

similar, it is difficult to keep track of the colours being used unless you apply the tesserae in a logical order.

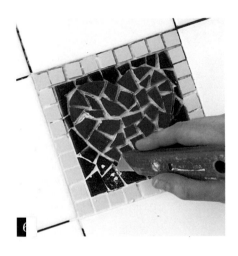

1 Use a permanent marker to draw or trace your design onto brown paper. Next, cut the yellow tile into small squares. To do this, first mark out a grid on the tile, using a water-soluble pen and a ruler. Here the tile is divided into 1.5cm (⅝in) squares. Score along all the marked lines with a tile cutter and breaker, pressing it against another tile to give you a straight line.

2 Use the tile cutter and breaker to cut along the score lines as shown, holding it in against the tile as far as it will go and lining up the pointer with the scored line. As you cut into the edge, the tile will break along the

entire line. First cut the tile into strips, and then cut the strips into squares. To get irregular-sized pieces (as with the red and blue ones here) either use nippers or bundle the tiles one at a time into a tea towel and smash them lightly with a hammer – be careful not to smash them to smithereens.

3 Working on one section at a time, apply washable PVA glue to the brown paper and then stick down the tesserae, making sure that they are stuck face down. This means that the wrong sides are face upwards, often all the same colour. Confusion can be avoided, however, by sticking the tesserae down in the right order. Leave to dry for approx. 12 hours.

4 Apply adhesive to your surface, in this case a wall, using a combed spatula or scraper to give even coverage of approx. 4mm (⅛in). Lay the paper-backed sheet of mosaic face down onto the adhesive-covered area aligning the edges correctly. Push down firmly using a block of wood or grout float to ensure that the mosaic beds into the adhesive securely. Leave to dry for approx. 24 hours.

5 Using warm water, dampen the brown paper to break down the washable PVA glue. Once damp, carefully peel the paper off the mosaic in one piece. If there is any resistance, dampen the paper further.

6 Rub the surface of the mosaic vigorously with a wet cloth to remove excess adhesive. If necessary, rake out stubborn areas of adhesive with a craft knife or other suitable tool. Finally, grout, clean and polish (see steps 5 and 6, page 21).

PROJECTS

Geometric mirror frame

THIS GEOMETRIC-STYLE BATHROOM MIRROR decorated in vitreous glass tesserae is very simple to make, and so it is suitable for complete beginners. There is little nipping required, because most of the tesserae are laid down whole, with only the tesserae for borders and edges cut in half, or quartered. It is also inexpensive, as the frame can be made cheaply from 18mm (¾in) MDF (medium-density fibreboard). We cut the frame ourselves for this project, but if you don't have the right equipment at home, most carpenters or DIY stores should be able to do it for you. Making an MDF frame has the advantage that you can get the exact size that you want – useful if you have a particular setting in mind. Remember, though, that it is very simple to adjust either the design or the spacing of the tesserae to fit your mosaic to an existing frame. An old or ugly frame would do perfectly well for this project, provided that the basic shape is suitable, because it will, of course, be completely covered in mosaic.

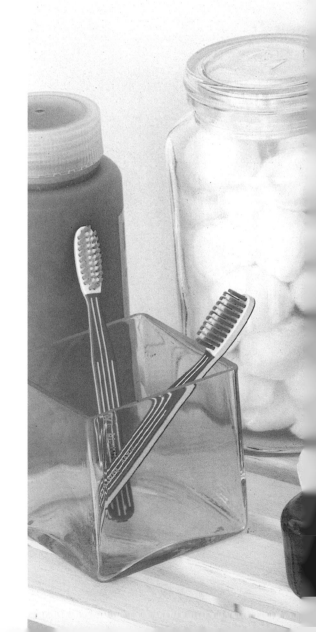

YOU WILL NEED

Basic Equipment (see page 20)

Tools
2.5cm (1in) artist's brush

Materials
Frame with border 8cm (3in) wide
Mirror
PVA sealer (1 part PVA to 4
   parts water)
1 litre (1¾pt) pot of ready-mixed
   water-resistant tile adhesive
Vitreous glass tesserae (Vetricolor):
   100 x green (20.58.2)
   100 x aqua (20.42.2)
   100 x grey (20.33.1)
   100 x white (20.10.1)
0.5kg (1lb) bag of ivory wide-
   joint grout
Small tube of silicone sealant

*If you have a ready-made frame
you'll also need:*
sandpaper
cardboard
masking tape

BASIC TECHNIQUES
(see pages 20–3)

ALTERNATIVE DESIGNS
(see pages 60–1)

The black-and-white template for this project is on page 78.

1 Seal the frame with PVA sealer to make it waterproof and leave it to dry for 60 minutes. If the frame is varnished or painted, sand the surface; if you are using a frame with a mirror

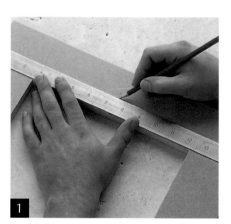

already in place, use cardboard and masking tape to cover and protect it. Measure the half-way point of each side of the frame and then draw a horizontal line across so that you are left with four quarters to work on, one at a time.

2 Cut an equal amount of each colour into halves for the inside edge and quarters for the inner border of the frame: cut around 12 of each colour to get the half-pieces (approx. 50), and 9 of each to get the quarter-pieces (approx. 35). To do this, position the nippers at the middle edge of the tessera and nip – the tessera should then snap into two halves. To get quarters, simply nip half-tesserae in half again. Starting in one corner, lay the tesserae in place to

use half-size tesserae for the outer edge as an alternative. Leave for approx. 24 hours until dry.

4 Grout, clean and polish (see steps 5 and 6, page 21). Turn the frame over and stick the mirror face down onto the back with silicone sealant. To do this accurately, position the mirror in place on the back of the frame and draw around it. Remove the mirror and then apply a thin bead of sealant between your drawn line and the edge of the frame. Re-position the mirror and secure in place with masking tape.

make sure that the pattern fits your frame. If it doesn't, you can easily adjust the amount of space (or grouting) between tesserae. You could, of course, adapt the design if you wish, adding or taking away a row or two of tesserae. Once you are happy with the layout you can start gluing.

3 Using your scraper, paste a quarter of the frame with the tile adhesive. Start sticking the tesserae firmly into place, working from the outer edge inwards to where the quarter-size tesserae form the inner border. Once you have completed one quarter of the frame, repeat the process until the whole frame is covered. Paste tile adhesive on the outside edge of the frame and cover with whole-size tesserae all the way round, lining up the colours with those on the face. Then place the half-size tesserae around the inside edge. You could

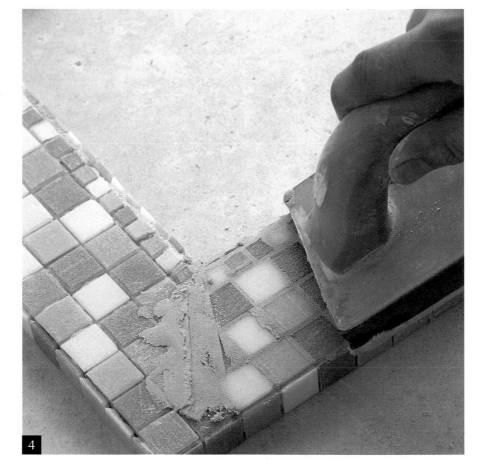

Classical-style lampbase

THE DESIGN FOR THIS LAMPBASE IS BOTH ELEGANT and simple, and the project is one of the easiest and quickest to make in the book. Its elegance lies in the use of only one colour and of the single repeated Roman-inspired fan motif. The subtle colouring means that the design relies on the motif itself and the pattern of the grouting or interstices to add interest and movement. This project illustrates well the role played by grouting in simplifying and stylizing mosaic design for maximum impact. The pale cream colour also means that this mosaic would sit well in most interiors, but if you would prefer a colourful lampbase, then the one featured on the jacket may inspire you; it uses exactly the same design as this one but in graduating shades of turquoise. The terracotta lampbase shape is a standard one, and is readily available from home stores. But don't worry if you can't get this exact lampbase, as it is easy to adapt the pattern to another shape. For safety reasons, make sure that no water gets into the hole for the electrical lead.

YOU WILL NEED

Basic Equipment (see page 20)

Tools
Water-soluble pen
Glass cutter
Tile cutter and breaker
  (see page 19)
Small pointing trowel

Materials
Lampbase approx. 28cm (11in) high
1 litre (1¾pt) pot of ready-mixed tile
  adhesive
Ceramic tiles 15cm x 15cm
  (6in x 6in):
    8 x satin cream
1.5kg (3lb) bag of ivory wide-
  joint grout

BASIC TECHNIQUES
(see pages 20–3)

ALTERNATIVE DESIGNS
(see pages 62–3)

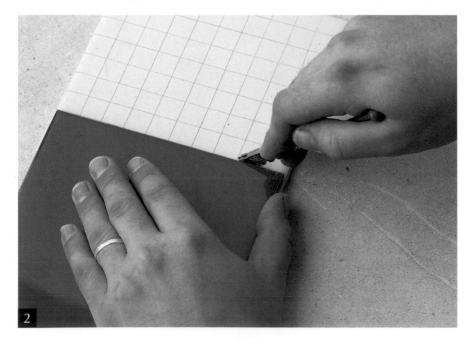

The black-and-white template for this project is on page 79.

1 In pencil, divide the lampbase, from top to bottom, into 5 equal bands to act as guidelines. Turn the lampbase on its side and pencil in 4 equal points around the circumference of the base. At each point draw an arc, or half a fan, and then continue upwards drawing in fan shapes.

2 Using a ruler and water-soluble pen, mark up approx. 8 tiles into 1.5cm (⅝in) squares. Use a glass cutter to score along the drawn lines, pressing it against the edge of another tile.

3 Cut along the scored lines using the tile cutter and breaker, first into strips and then into squares (see page 23). To do this, position the tile in the teeth of the breaker, aligning the pointer with the scored line and pushing it up as far as it will go, then grasp the handles together to cut the tile cleanly.

4 Using the small pointing trowel, apply adhesive to each marked fan shape in turn, and stick down the tesserae in rows, working from the outer curve inwards. The final tessera in each fan shape will need to be cut into a triangle to fit the V-shaped tip (see page 20). Leave to dry for 24 hours, then grout, clean and polish (see steps 5 and 6, page 21).

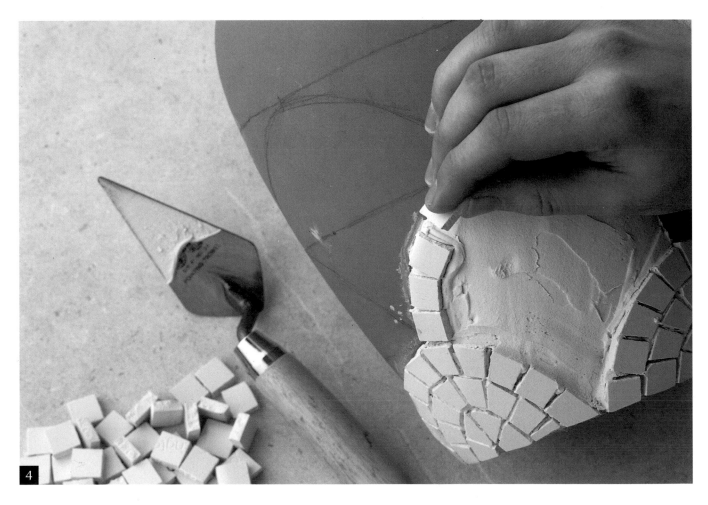

Kitsch kitchen vase

ANOTHER QUICK AND EASY PROJECT AND PROBABLY the most fun and colourful, inspired by the gaudy flower prints of the late Sixties and early Seventies. It is made up of ceramic tiles, cut into small tesserae, combined with glass beads, and so would be ideal for using up old or reject tiles. Patterned tiles or smashed crockery could also be used, but give some thought to how the patterns and colours work together so as not to lose contrast or definition. To heighten colour, a bright green grout is used – coloured grouts can either be bought ready-made, or made up by adding poster paint to a neutral-coloured grout; they are a good way of enlivening mosaic pieces. When working with a 3-D form such as this, it is important to keep the tesserae small so that they don't protrude and the surface is kept as smooth as possible. You could use any shape or size of vase (though the instructions on the following pages obviously relate to the one shown) and any other 3-D object – such as a lampbase, sculpture or statue.

YOU WILL NEED

Basic Equipment (see page 20)

Tools
Tile cutter and breaker (see page 19)

Materials
Vase, approx. 24cm (9½in) high
1 litre (1¾pt) pot of ready-mixed
  water-resistant tile adhesive
Ceramic tiles 15cm x 15cm
  (6in x 6in)
    3 x shades of green
    2 x yellow
    2 x orange
    2 x white
10 coloured glass beads
1.5kg (3lb) bag of white wide-
  joint grout plus green poster paint
  or 1.5kg (3lb) bag of green grout

BASIC TECHNIQUES
(see pages 20–3)

ALTERNATIVE DESIGNS
(see pages 64–5)

The black-and-white template for this project is on page 80.

1 Cut the tiles into strips, some 1cm (½in) and some 2cm (¾in) wide (see steps 1 and 2, page 23), then nip these into rough wedge shapes or triangles to give a variety of petal sizes. Nip the green tiles into small irregular shaped pieces, no larger than 1cm (½in) square. These will be used to fill in the spaces between the flowers.

2 Glass beads are used for some of the flower centres, but to add variety of texture and size, cut up a few tile pieces into circular shapes. To do this, hold a 1cm (½in) square piece of tile in one hand and nip at the corners with the other hand, turning as you do so, until you get a rough circular shape.

3 Paste up a roughly tile-sized area of the vase at a time. Stick down a flower middle, and then arrange the wedge-shaped petals around it. If the petal pieces are too long, they will jut out and form sharp, protruding edges. If this is the case, nip your petals down a little. For our vase, we stuck down about 3 flowers at a time, overlapping some of them, so that part of some of the flowers appears to be hidden behind others.

4 Fill the areas between the flowers with green pieces. Repeat the process until the entire surface of the vase is covered. Clean off any excess adhesive with a damp sponge and leave to dry for 24 hours before grouting. The green grout used here can either be bought, or made up by mixing poster paint with white grout, but be careful not to stain your clothes or furniture. Grout, clean and polish (see steps 5 and 6, page 21).

Silver star picture frame

THE COMBINATION OF SILVER LEAF WITH WHITE porcelain tesserae in a simple design creates a stylish, contemporary look. This is not the least expensive project – silver tesserae are costly as they are made with silver leaf – but only small amounts are needed here so the expense is kept down. And the silver makes all the difference, as it catches the light and contrasts with the opaque porcelain. You can use gold if you prefer, although this is also expensive; and if keeping costs to a minimum is a priority, then you can try pieces of mirror glass instead of silver. To make the frame you (or your local joiner or timber merchant) will need to do the following: cut a 30cm (1ft) square out of 18mm (¾in) MDF, and then cut a circle 17.5cm (7in) diameter from the centre. Out of the back rout a 20cm (8in) square around the circle for the glass and picture to sit in. Alternatively, you could mosaic an existing frame, but you would need to sand it down and seal it with PVA sealer. The direct method is used here but the indirect method would also be possible.

YOU WILL NEED

Basic Equipment (see page 20)

Tools
Compass
Water-soluble pen
Glass cutter
Tile cutter and breaker (see page 19)

Materials
Picture frame 30cm x 30cm
   (1ft x 1ft)
PVA sealer (1 part PVA to 4 parts
   water)
1 litre (1¾pt) pot of ready-mixed
   water-resistant tile adhesive
80 x silver leaf mosaic tesserae
   20mm x 20mm (¾in x ¾in)
150 x white porcelain tesserae
   25mm x 25mm (1in x 1in)
1.5kg (3lb) bag of white wide-
   joint grout

BASIC TECHNIQUES

(see pages 20–3)

ALTERNATIVE DESIGNS

(see pages 66–7)

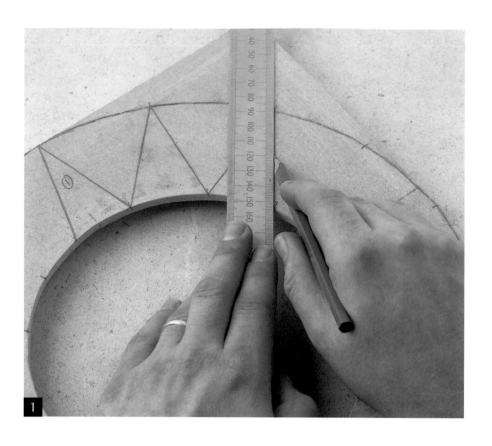

the outer edge and working inwards. You'll need to nip them into smaller, triangular pieces as you get to the bottom of each V shape. To fill the remaining 4 corners, paste up each in turn and stick down the tesserae, again following the circular pattern. As in step 2, lay each tessera over the edge of the picture frame, score and cut. Make sure the tesserae do not overhang the frame edge.

4 To tile the inner and outer edges in white, you'll need to measure the thickness of your frame. For this frame, the half-tesserae are the right size for the outer edge. For the inside edge, hold the tesserae upright against the edge, mark the necessary thickness in pencil and then score and cut along the line. In order to make sure that the tesserae do not hang below where the glass will go, turn the frame over and press down with a tile to make sure that everything is level. Cut all the pieces you need (approx. 20) into halves, and then apply adhesive to each edge before sticking down. Once complete, clean the mosaic with a damp sponge and leave to dry for 24 hours. Then grout, clean and polish (see steps 5 and 6, page 21), and replace the glass in the frame.

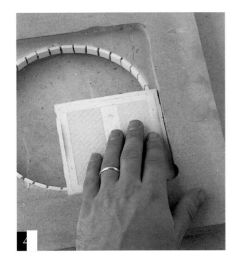

around this circle at slightly irregular intervals so that the spikes vary in size. Draw in the spikes, using the template as a guide, joining the 16 points to another 16 marked on the inner edge.

2 If you are using a frame the same size as ours, you will find that the length of each spike uses about 3 silver-leaf tesserae. To cut the tesserae so that they fit the spike shape, lay them on the spike and mark with the water-soluble pen where the lines of the spike run under the tile. Score with the glass cutter, break with the tile cutter and breaker, and then stick the tesserae down, one spike at a time.

The black-and-white template for this project is on page 81.

1 Remove the glass from your frame and put it in a safe place. Seal the frame with PVA sealer and leave to dry. Using the compass, draw a circle that fills the frame, touching the outer edge at each side. Mark 16 points

3 Cut the porcelain tesserae into quarters using the nippers, and don't worry if they are slightly irregular. Apply adhesive to each inverse spike and stick the tesserae down in a circular pattern, starting at

Mediterranean-style dish

SMALL SQUARE TESSERAE ARE CAREFULLY GRADUATED to create a sea of aquamarine as a background for these golden-coloured fish. They are made up of irregularly shaped pieces so that each one looks different. The entire mosaic is made with vitreous glass tesserae which are not only particularly suitable for colour fades, but are also thin enough not to add too much weight or bulk to the dish. This is an easy design to follow but it will still take up to a day in total to complete because the adhesive needs to be left to dry overnight. This is always the case when glass is applied to a glazed surface and means that you need to take special care when cleaning off excess adhesive from the tesserae before they are completely set. The original dish was highly patterned, as you can see in the step-by-step photographs overleaf, and in fact was sold as a reject – a reminder that mosaic covers a multitude of sins and can give a new lease of life to objects that are faulty or ugly. As this is a 3-D project the direct method is used.

YOU WILL NEED

Basic Equipment (see page 20)

Tools
Permanent marker
Scissors

Materials
Platter dish 38cm (15in) in diameter
Stiff paper or card
1 litre (1¾pt) pot of ready-mixed
 tile adhesive
Vitreous glass tesserae (Vetricolor):
 85 x very light aqua (20.35.2)
 65 x light aqua (20.42.2)
 55 x aqua (20.57.2)
 45 x dark aqua (20.67.2)
 30 x dark orange (20.99.3)
 30 x light orange (20.79.3)
1.5kg (3lb) bag grey wide-
 joint grout

BASIC TECHNIQUES
(see pages 20–3)

ALTERNATIVE DESIGNS
(see pages 68–9)

The black-and-white template for this project is on page 82.

1 Using a permanent marker, draw 8 lines from the centre of the bowl outwards to give you 8 equal segments. Mark 3 equal points along each line and then join up to create 3 concentric circles. These will be your guidelines for positioning the tesserae.

2 Draw and cut out a simple fish motif from stiff paper or card, about the size of the one shown here. On each of the 8 lines, and on the outermost guideline, draw around the motif to end up with 8 fish, all pointing in the same direction.

3 Nip the two shades of orange tesserae into small irregular pieces, then paste up and fill in the fish shapes, keeping to the drawn outlines, one at a time. Nip some of the tesserae into triangular-shaped pieces in order to form the head and tail.

3

4 To fill in the blue background, start with approx. 5 rows of the darkest colour in the centre. Then work outwards, fading gradually from dark to light. Graduate as follows: for every 3 tesserae of the darker shade on a row, add a single tessera of the lighter; then, on the next row, for every 3 of the lighter shade, add a single darker one. Then fill in 2–3 solid lines of the lighter shade – and so on until the entire surface is covered. When you reach the fish motifs, you will have to nip the tesserae into triangular or wedge-shaped pieces to fit around them. Clean off excess adhesive with a damp sponge before leaving to dry for 24 hours. Finally, grout, clean and polish (see steps 5 and 6, page 21).

4

African-style tabletop

Primitive African tribal paintings inspired this bold, simple design and vibrant colour scheme. This is not a difficult design, but the project will take up to two days to complete because of the length of time needed for the PVA glue to dry. Ceramic tiles are widely available everywhere but most of those used here were picked up in tile clearance shops or at car boot sales. These are excellent places for the bargain hunter because even the ugliest tiles have potential, as the gaudy orange tiles used here prove. Charcoal grout unifies the piece and adds to its impact, but take care because it does stain easily when wet. The top, 60cm (2ft) in diameter, was cut from 25mm (1in) MDF: a local joiner or timber merchant could easily do this for you. This base was made by a local blacksmith but ready-made bases are widely available. Alternatively, you could mosaic an existing table. For a project like this, where the tiles are of different thicknesses, it is easier to use the indirect method, which allows you to get the flat surface needed for a tabletop.

YOU WILL NEED

Basic Equipment (see page 20)

Tools
Craft knife
2.5cm (1in) artist's brush
Scissors
Tea towel
Hammer
Glass cutter
Tile cutter and breaker (see page 19)
Combed scraper or spatula
Block of wood

Materials
Tabletop 60cm (2ft) in diameter,
 cut from 25mm (1in) thick MDF
PVA sealer (1 part PVA to 4
 parts water)
Brown paper
Washable PVA glue (1 part PVA
 glue to 3 parts water)
Ceramic tiles 15cm x 15cm
 (6in x 6in)
  6 x mottled brown
  3 x plain orange
  3 x mottled orange
  13 x black
  2 x bronze
1 litre (1¾pt) pot of ready-mixed
 water-resistant tile adhesive
1.5kg (3lb) bag of charcoal wide-
 joint grout

BASIC TECHNIQUES
(see pages 20–3)

ALTERNATIVE DESIGNS
(see pages 70–1)

The black-and-white template for this project is on page 83.

1 Using the craft knife, key the entire surface of the tabletop and then seal with PVA sealer, using the artist's brush. Leave to dry. Cut out a piece of brown paper the exact size of the tabletop. Keep aside approx. 1 bronze tile and 5 black tiles for the table edge. To get the irregular black and orange pieces you need for the surface, bundle the tiles up, one at a time, into a tea towel and smash lightly with a hammer. Go easy on this; you want to end up with large and small coin-sized pieces, not smithereens. Remember to keep the different colours in three separate piles, to avoid confusion.

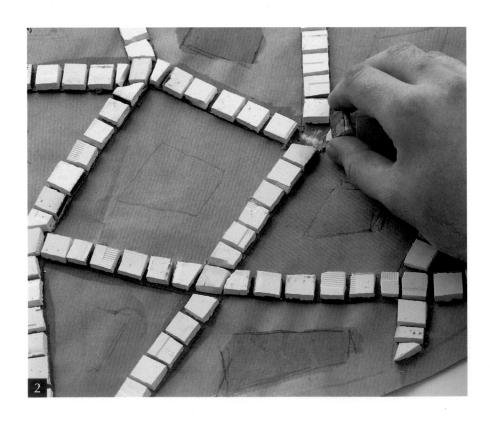

2 Draw approx. 25 irregular diamond shapes, approx.10cm (4in) square, over the paper, with smaller, similar shapes in the centre of each. Using the tile cutter and breaker, cut the brown and bronze tiles into strips 1.5cm (⅝in) wide, then cut approx. 4 of the bronze strips, and all the brown strips, into 1cm (½in) squares (see page 23). Using washable PVA glue, stick the brown tesserae face down, and then position the bronze tesserae to fit the space where the lines intersect. Note that all the tesserae will appear white as they are upside-down, but if you stick them down in the right order – the brown first, and then the bronze – you won't get confused.

3 Apply glue to each irregular square. Stick down the orange tesserae first, mixing the shades, then fill in the surrounding area with black.

3

4 Once the mosaic has dried on the paper, you can transfer it to the tabletop. Using a combed scraper or spatula, paste up the surface of the tabletop, then turn upside down and place on top of the mosaic. Push down firmly, using the block of wood. When dry, after approx. 24 hours, turn over, dampen the brown paper and peel it off. Remove any excess glue by rubbing with a wet cloth, using the craft knife to gouge out any stubborn areas if necessary. Next, cut the remaining black and bronze tiles into strips the thickness of the edge. Stick these down all around the edge, lining up the bronze strips with the bronze tesserae on the surface. Some of the tops of these strips will be white, but the charcoal grout will stain them black. Leave to dry for 24 hours, then grout, clean and polish (see steps 5 and 6, page 21).

4

Pebble urn for outdoors

THIS PROJECT WITH ITS CLASSIC PEBBLE DECORATION was especially designed for the garden, and so a large frostproof terracotta urn and exterior-quality powder-mix adhesive were used. The limited use of smalti for the zigzag motif, combined with porcelain tesserae and pebbles, keeps the cost of this project down. The pebbles are, of course, free and can be collected from beaches, parks or gardens: choose small, smooth stones, and aim for a mixture of grey and white to match the colours of the mosaic. The design is simple and easy to follow but it will take time to cover the large surface area, and it is worth taking care when drawing the zigzag motif, making sure that it joins up well. To achieve a good finish, clean as you go along, taking care not to snag the smalti or pebbles. Leave it to dry totally, then wash and scrub using a scourer and a phosphoric acid-based cleaner before rinsing with clean water. The white-painted rim tones in well, but you could stick with the terracotta, or try a rich colour, such as blue or green, for a brighter look.

YOU WILL NEED

Basic Equipment (see page 20)

Tools
2.5cm (1in) artist's brush
Scissors

Materials
Terracotta urn 30cm (12in) high
  (frostproof if for outdoor use)
PVA sealer (1 part PVA to 4
  parts water)
Stiff paper or card
I litre (1¾pt) pot of adhesive
  (or 5kg [11lb] bag of exterior-
  quality powder-mix adhesive
  if for outdoor use)
White eggshell paint
Small pebbles
Smalti:
  50 x dark blue (69)
  50 x light blue (70)
Porcelain tesserae 25mm x 25mm
  (1in x 1in):
    150 x grey-blue (112)
1.5kg (3lb) bag white
  wide-joint grout

BASIC TECHNIQUES
(see pages 20–3)

ALTERNATIVE DESIGNS
(see pages 72–3)

The black-and-white template for this project is on page 84.

1 Seal the urn with PVA sealer, using the artist's brush. To make a V-shaped template for the zigzag, first cut all the blue smalti into halves. Lay them out in an arrowhead shape on stiff paper or card, then draw around the shape and cut out. Draw a line on the urn where the bottom of the zigzag will be, and a second, parallel line 8cm (3in) above it, to create a strip in which to draw the zigzag.

2 Align the template with the marked lines on the urn, and draw around it to mark a zigzag all around the urn.

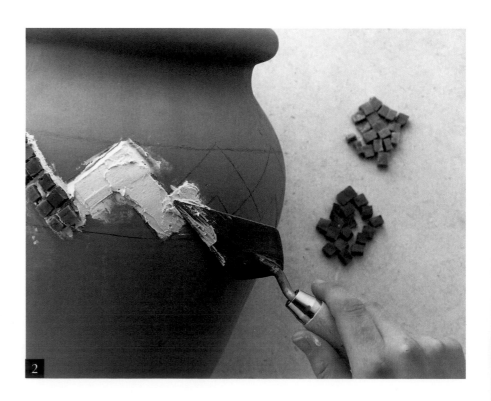

Paste up the zigzag area, and stick down the tesserae in sections so that the adhesive does not dry out.

3 Cut the grey porcelain tesserae into quarters. Starting at the bottom of the urn, apply adhesive in bands and stick down the tesserae; in this way the adhesive will be prevented from drying out. Continue in this way until you reach the zigzag. Here you will have to cut the quarters into triangles to fit (see page 20). Clean off any excess adhesive as you go along, being careful not to move the tesserae.

If you wait until you have completely finished sticking them down before you do this, the adhesive may dry hard and will be difficult to remove.

4 Before you mosaic above the zigzag line, paint the rim of the pot in white eggshell paint and leave to dry. You could, of course, choose another colour for the rim: grey or pale blue would be obvious alternatives for matching the colour scheme. Paste up small areas at a time with generous amounts of adhesive, and then stick down the pebbles, spacing them out roughly as shown. Once you have finished, clean the surface of the pebbles – as in step 3. Leave the mosaic to dry for 24 hours, then grout, clean and polish (see steps 5 and 6, page 21) to finish.

Half-moon tabletop

THIS ELEGANT CONSOLE TABLETOP, WITH ITS SUBDUED colour scheme and subtle border patterns, should suit a range of interiors and tastes. It has perhaps the most intricate of our project designs and so complete beginners may not want to start off with this one. The indirect method is recommended for this project as it enables you to follow the drawn design more easily (see page 22). The tabletop needs to be cut (either by yourself, a local joiner or timber merchant) from 25mm (1in) MDF as follows: cut a semi-circle with a diameter of 90cm (3ft); draw a line 65mm (2½in) in from − and parallel to − the straight edge of the diameter, and cut along it. You should now have the truncated semi-circle shape you need for this project. These chic aluminium legs came from a company that specializes in aluminium casting, but you could buy a ready-made base or have one made. The project will take up to two days to complete because of the length of time the PVA glue takes to dry before you can transfer the mosaic to the tabletop.

YOU WILL NEED

Basic Equipment (see page 20)

Tools

Craft knife
2.5cm (1in) artist's brush
Scissors
Water-soluble pen
Glass cutter
Tile cutter and breaker (see page 19)
Combed scraper or spatula
Squeegee or block of wood

Materials

Tabletop, 90cm (3ft) long at
  straight edge, cut from 25mm
  (1in) thick MDF
PVA sealer (1 part PVA to 4
  parts water)
Brown paper
Washable PVA glue (1 part PVA
  glue to 3 parts water)
Vitreous glass tesserae (Vetricolor):
  200 x white gold vein (Le Gemme
    20.20.4)
  80 x Russet Gold Blend
  55 x gold (20.10.4)
Porcelain tesserae 25mm x 25mm
  (1in x 1in):
  200 x old rose
  100 x beige
1 litre (1¾pt) pot of ready-mixed
  water-resistant tile adhesive
1.5kg (3lb) bag of ivory wide-
  joint grout

BASIC TECHNIQUES

(see pages 20–3)

ALTERNATIVE DESIGNS

(see pages 74–5)

The black-and-white template for this project is on page 85.

1 Using the craft knife, score the MDF tabletop and seal with PVA sealer, including the edges and underneath, using the artist's brush. Leave to dry for 1 hour, or until the surface is completely dry. Lay the tabletop on a sheet of brown paper, draw around it and cut out. Use a porcelain tessera to gauge the width of the outer border and draw a line all around.

2 From the line you have drawn, you are going to draw the remaining 3 guidelines. To do this, measure in approx. 3½ glass tesserae, 4 porcelain tesserae and then 3½ glass tesserae. Now draw in the 2 wavy lines as shown below, using the template as a guide if necessary. Brush washable PVA glue onto the outer edge of the brown paper. Stick down the outside ring of porcelain tiles face down, mixing the two shades. When this is done, leave a 2mm (1/16in) grout gap

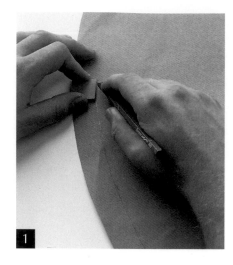

before you start the next border. Remember that you will need to leave a gap between each row of tesserae.

3 Starting with the wavy line, paste and stick down a continuous line of white tesserae, smooth side down. Beneath and above the wavy line, you will have a series of semi-circular shapes which you should mosaic one at a time. Follow the template to work outwards from the wavy line. First stick

down half-tesserae of the Russet Gold Blend, then more white and finally the gold tesserae (see step 4), always allowing a 2mm (¹⁄₁₆in) grout gap. You will sometimes need to cut the tesserae into wedge shapes to make them fit (see page 20).

4 When you come to the edge and are filling in the gold-coloured tiles, hold them over the edge, mark where they need cutting using the water-soluble pen, and score with a glass cutter or tile cutter and breaker and then break, using the latter. Continue this process until the whole border is finished. Repeat the whole process for the inner border.

To complete the project:

To fill in the remaining areas with a mix of the two shades of porcelain tesserae, first count and put aside the amount needed for the table edge (approx. 50) and for the middle border (approx. 150). Cut the remaining tiles into quarters. Paste up the centre and stick down the quarters in straight lines. Finally paste up and fill in the area between the wavy borders with full-size pieces in a circular pattern. Leave to dry for 24 hours. Using a combed spatula or scraper, paste the table surface with water-resistant adhesive, then turn upside down and place on top of the mosaic, ensuring that the curved edges align. Firmly press down with a squeegee or block of wood. Paste up the table edge and, mixing the two shades, stick down the whole porcelain tiles. Leave to dry for 24 hours. Soak the brown paper with a damp sponge and peel off in one piece. Clean off excess adhesive with a wet cloth. Finally grout, clean, and polish (see steps 5 and 6, page 21).

ALTERNATIVE DESIGNS

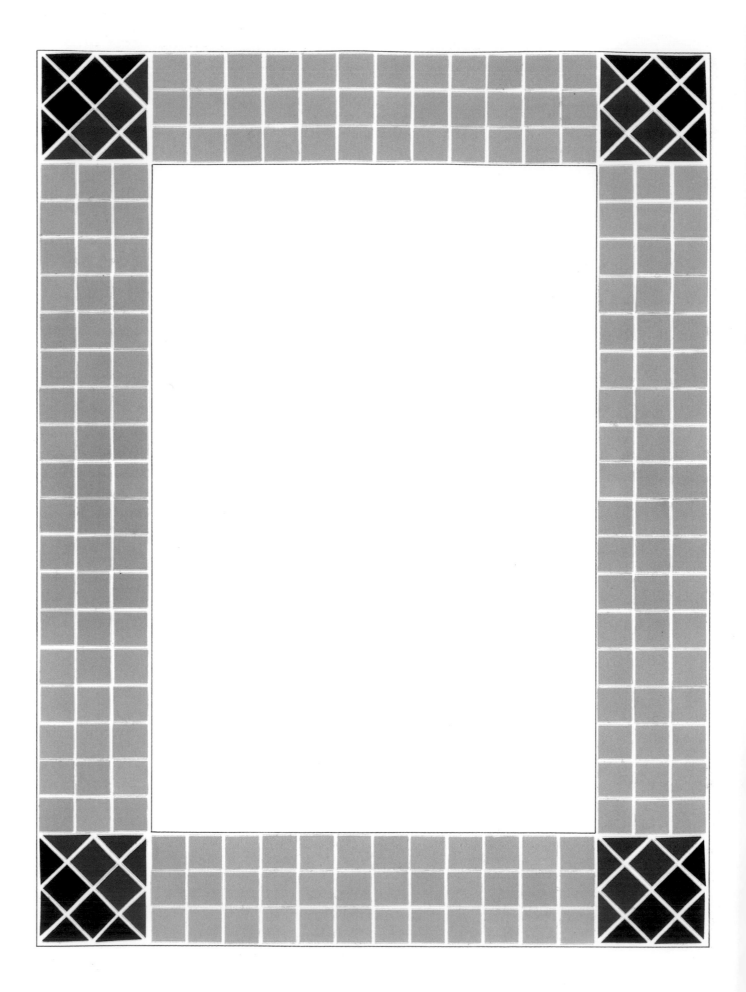

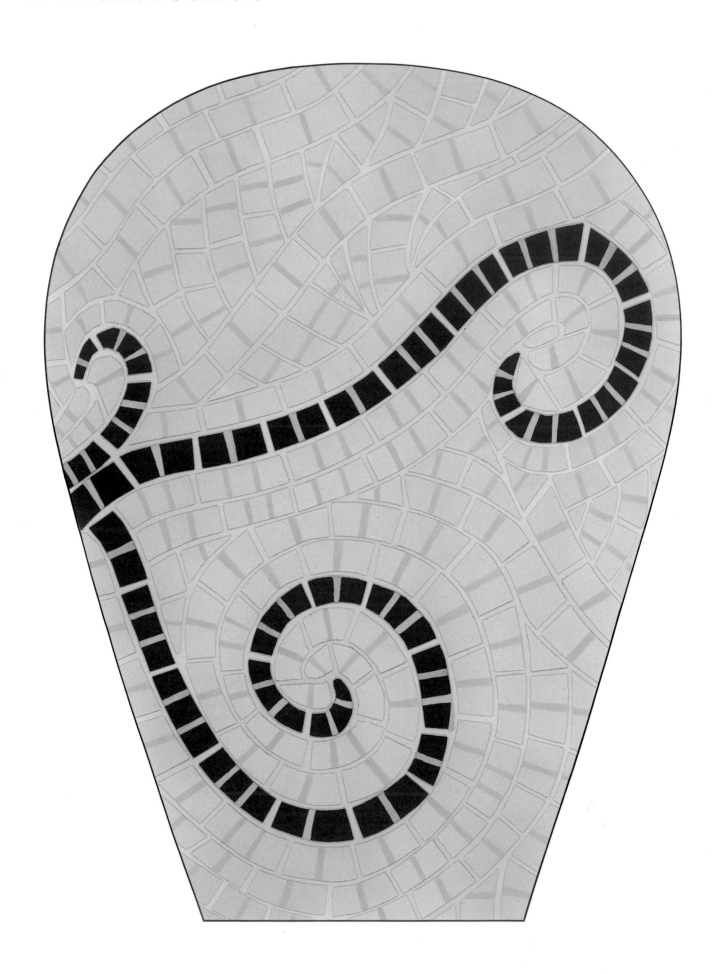

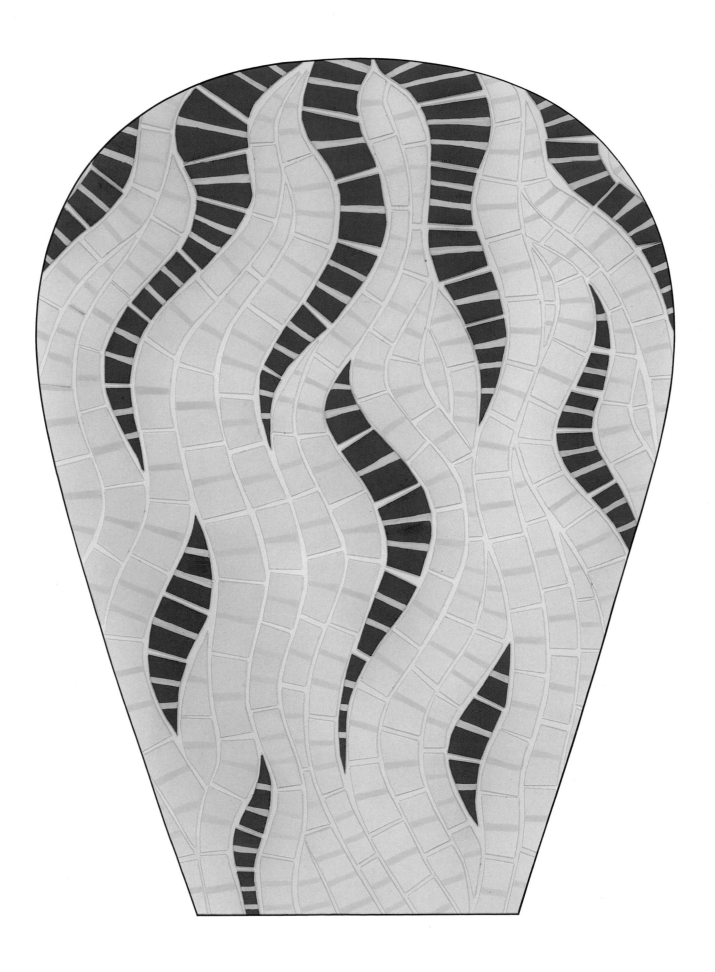

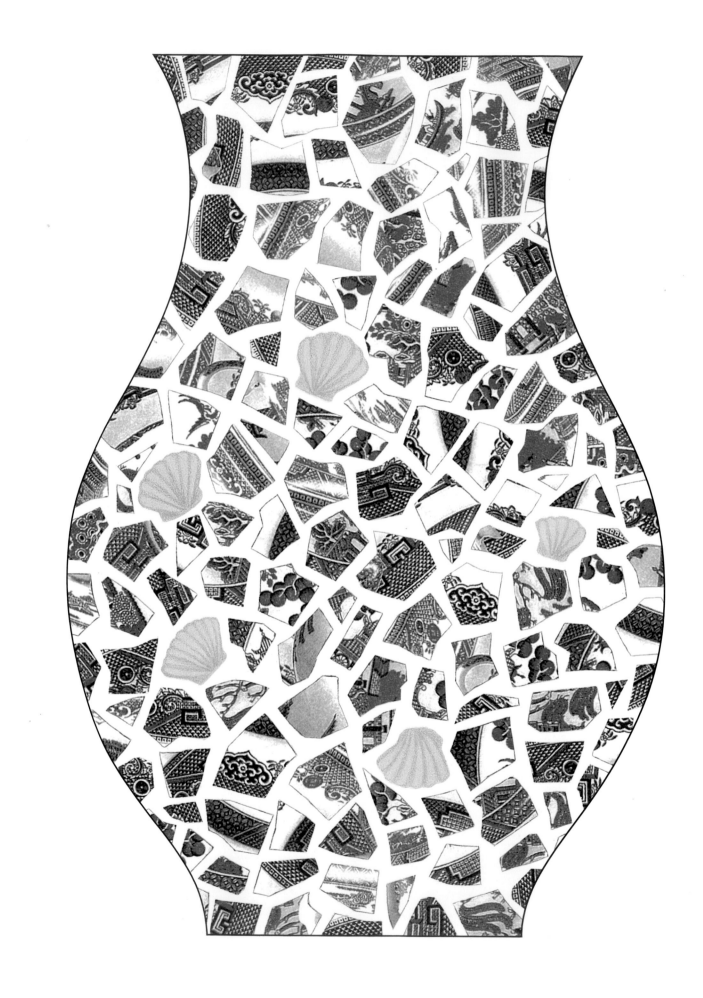

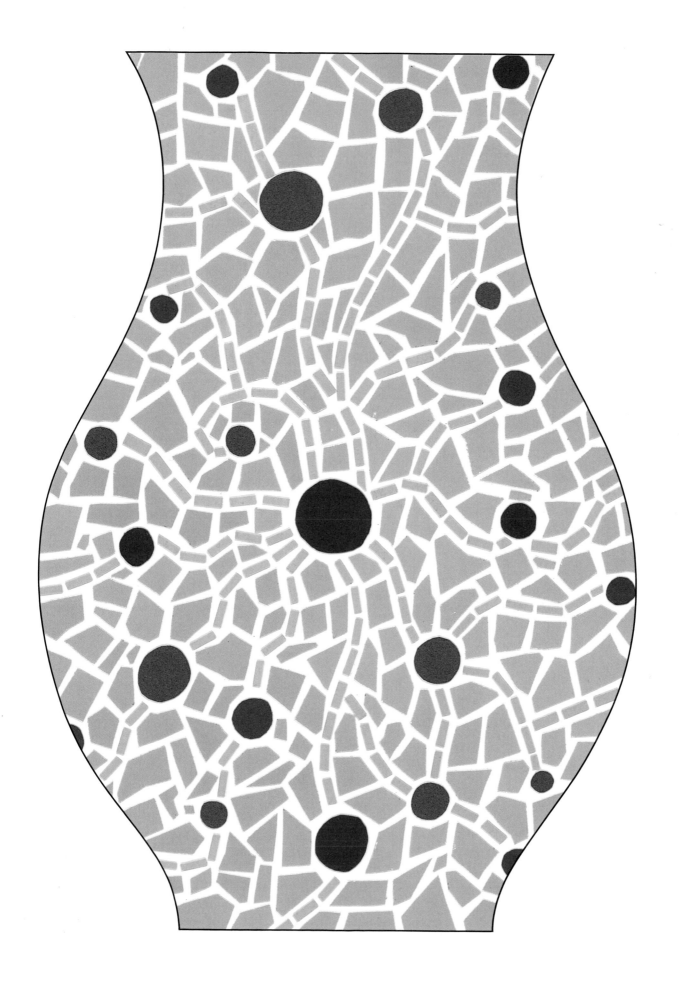

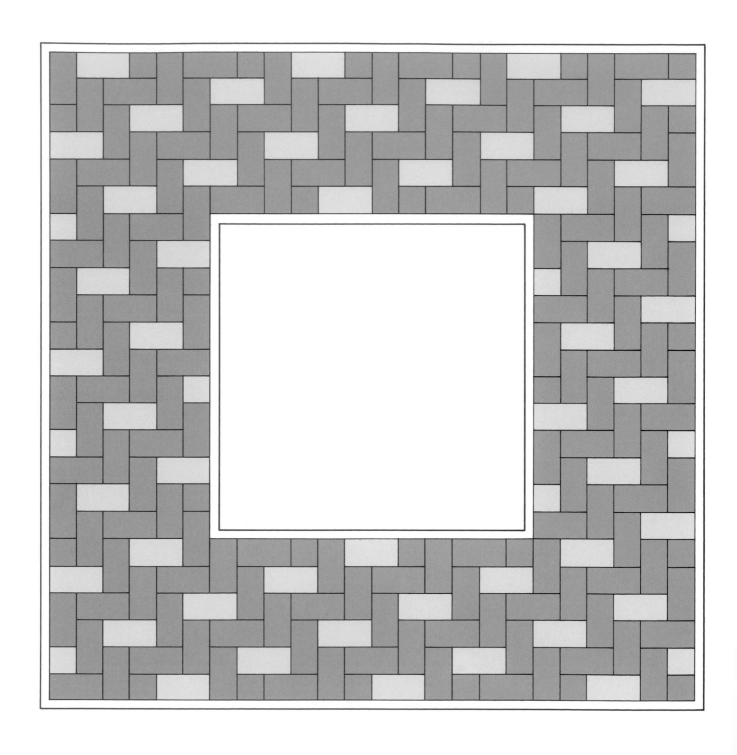

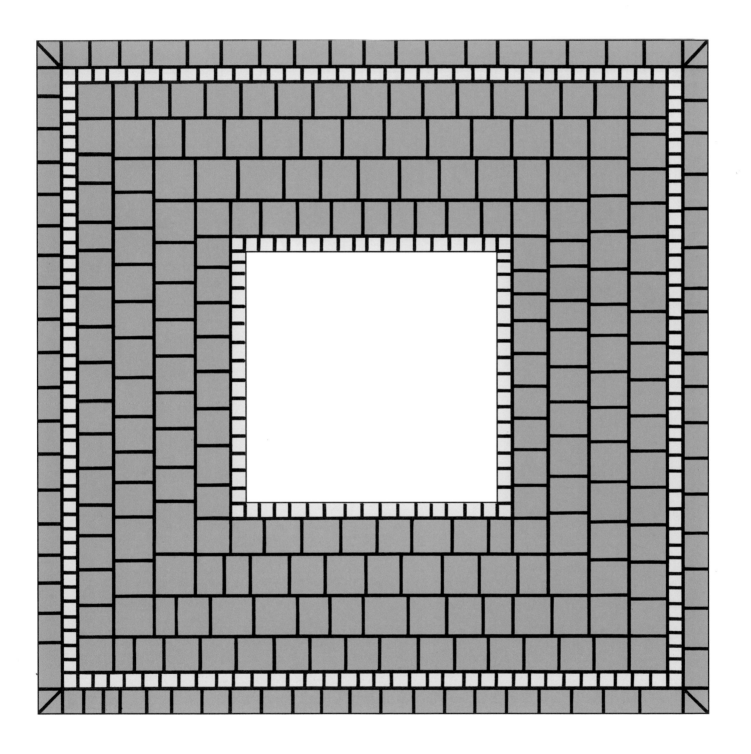

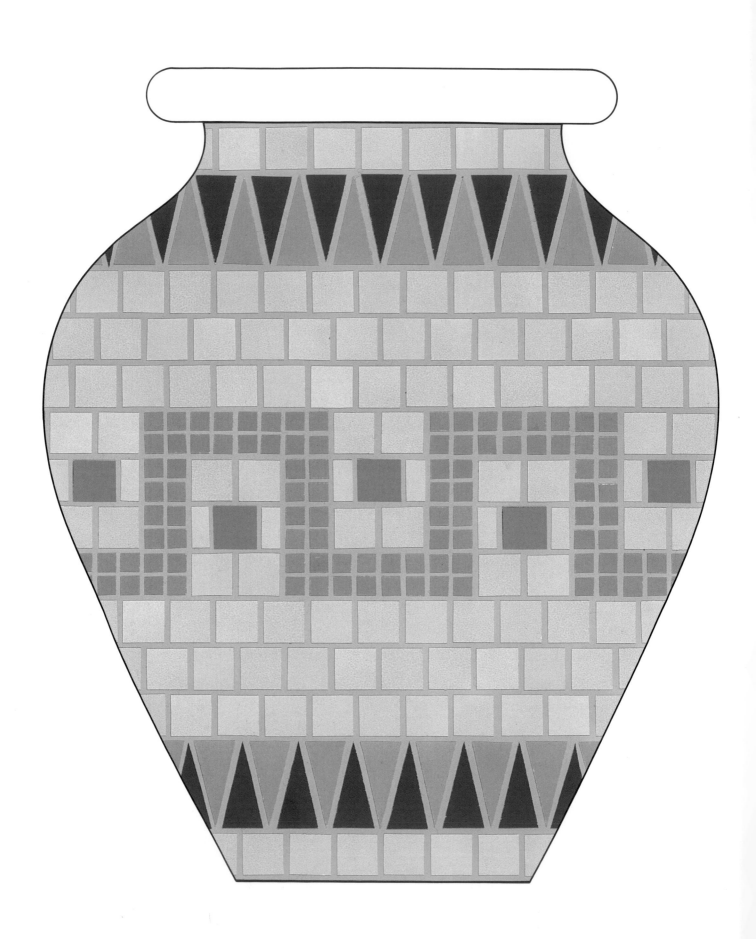

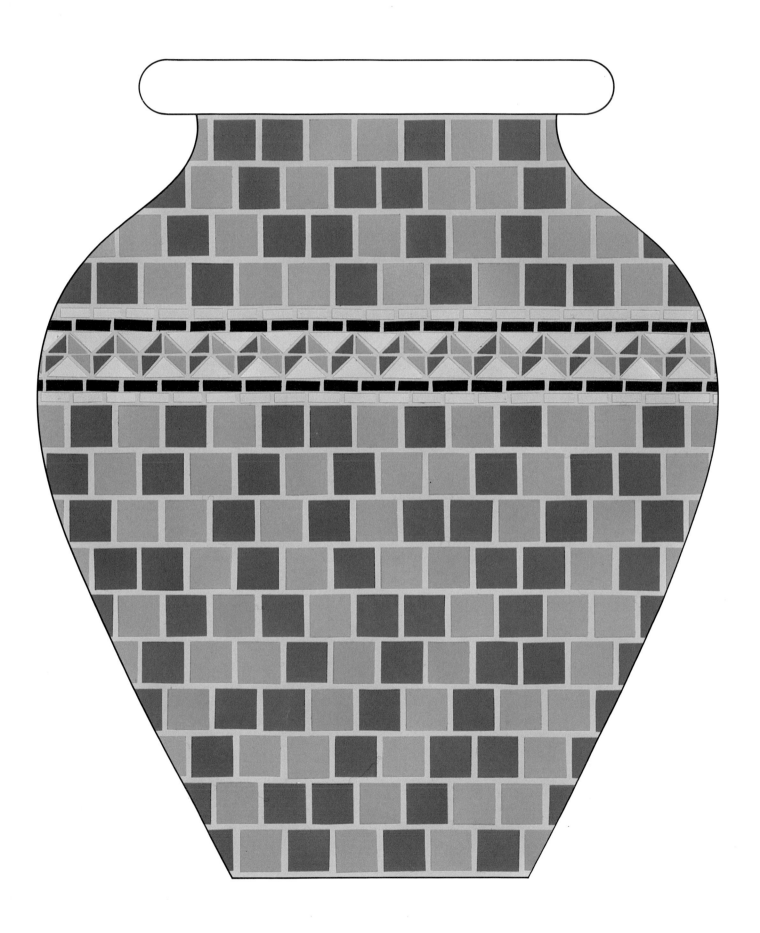

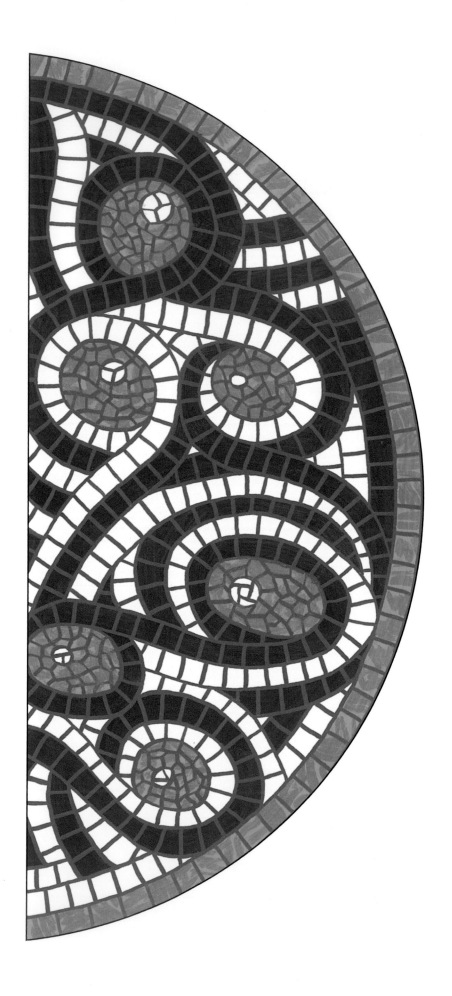

TEMPLATES
& MOTIFS

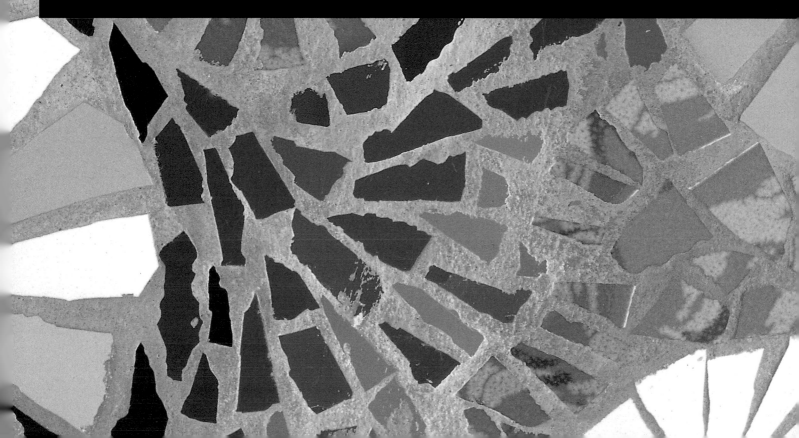

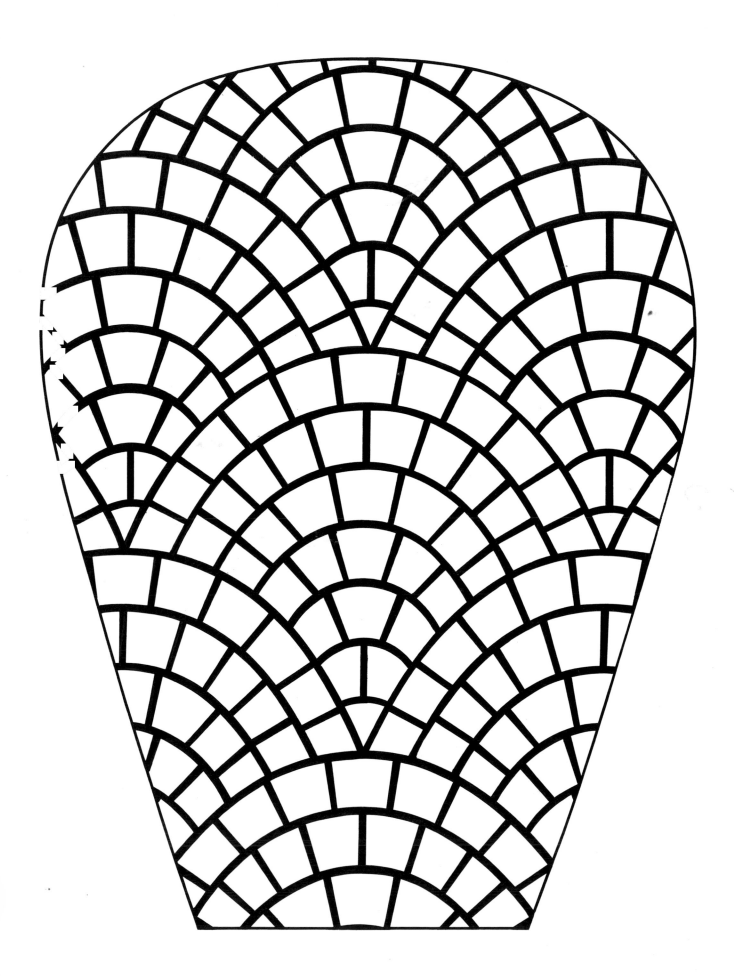

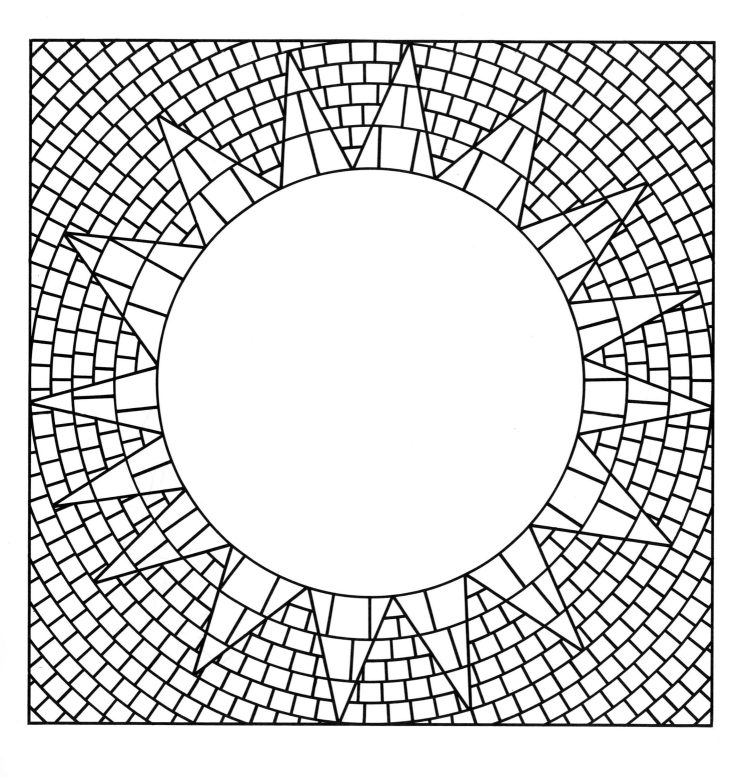

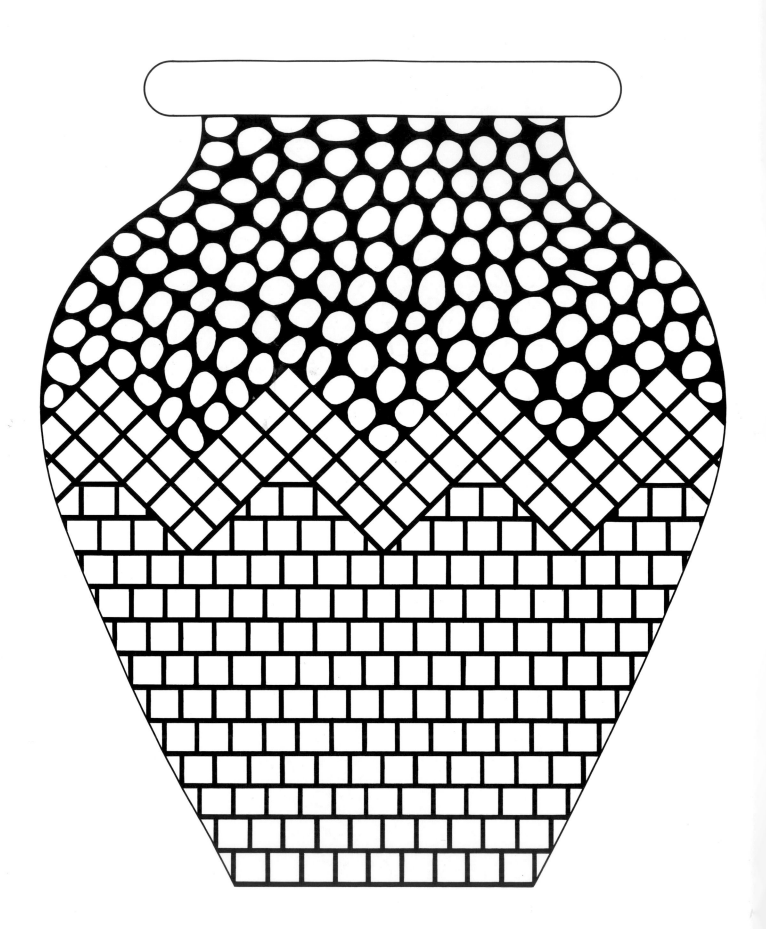

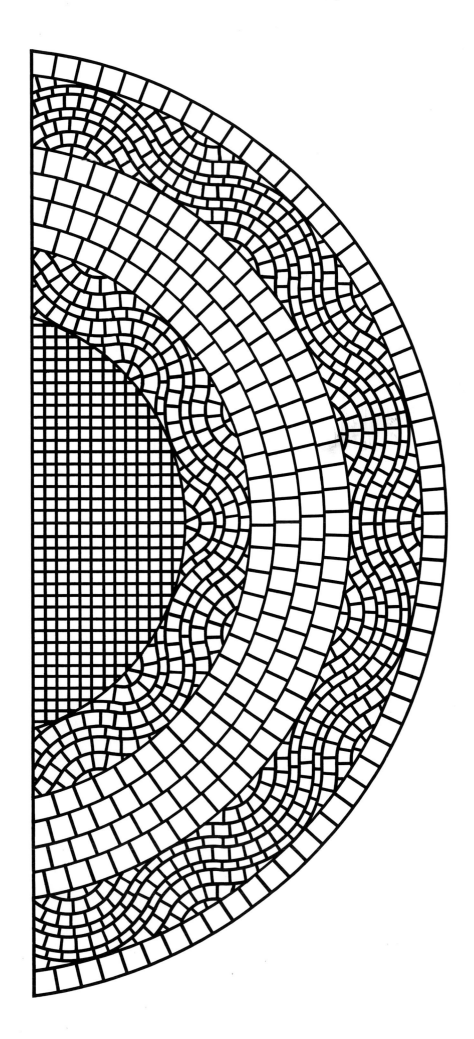

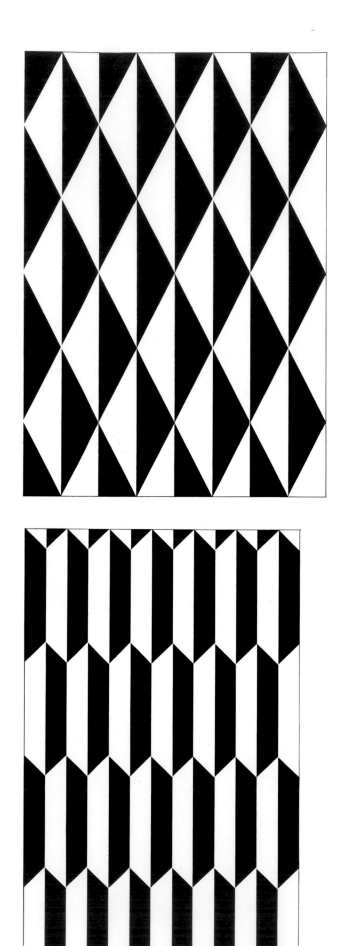

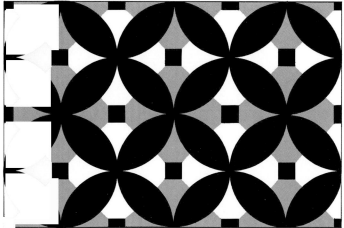

UNITED KINGDOM

The Mosaic Studio supply glass and porcelain tesserae, and mosaic tools and equipment. In addition to supplying mail-order mosaics and mosaics by commission, they also run weekend courses on the art of mosaic.

The Mosaic Studio
159 Southsea Avenue
Leigh-on-Sea
Essex SS9 2BH
Tel: 01702 712111

Edgar Udny & Co Ltd
314 Balham High Road
London SW17 7AA
Tel: 0181 767 8181
Mosaic tools and materials. Large selection of vitreous glass, ceramic and porcelain tesserae

James Hetley & Co Ltd
Glasshouse Fields
London E1 9JA
Tel: 0171 790 2333
Coloured glass. Mail order available

Paul Fricker Ltd
Well Park
Willeys Avenue
Exeter
Devon EX2 8BE
Tel: 01392 278636

Reed Harris Ltd
Riverside House
Carnwath Road
London SW6 3HR
Tel: 0171 736 7511
Marble and ceramic tiles

Tower Ceramics
91 Parkway
Camden Town
London NW1 7PP
Tel: 0171 485 7192
Importers of ceramic tiles; stockists of adhesives, grout and cleaning products for marble and terracotta

The Mosaic Workshop
Unit B, 443–9 Holloway Road
London N7 6LJ
Tel: 0171 263 2997
A range of mosaic materials, tools and tesserae. Mail-order mosaics and mosaics to commission

CANADA

Interstyle Ceramic and Glass Ltd
8051 Enterprise St., Burnaby
Vancouver B.C.
Canada V5A 1V5
Toll Free Telephone and Fax: 1 800 667 1566

AUSTRALIA

Academy Tiles
20 Herbert Street
Artarmon, NSW 2064
Tel: (02) 9436 3566

Architectural and Designer Centre
664 Botany Road
Alexandria, NSW 2015
Tel: (02) 9669 6211

Erneste Ceramics Imports
1281-3 Sydney Road
Fawkner, VIC 3060
Tel: (03) 9359 6533

Romano Tiles
Factory 3 & 4
126 Canterbury Road
Kilsyth, VIC 3137
Tel: (03) 9720 4633

SOUTH AFRICA

Duratile
North Reef Road
Bedfordview
Johannesburg
Tel: (011) 455 5500

Home Warehouse (Pty) Ltd
Vickers Street
City Deep
Johannesburg
Tel: (011) 613 7111

Just Tiles
6 Vickers Road
City Deep
Johannesburg
Tel: (011) 613 6751

Omega Tiles (Pty) Ltd
Hammer Avenue
Strijdom Park
Randburg
Tel: (011) 792 6870

Roma Tile (Pty) Ltd
53 Innes Road
Jet Park, Ext. 6
Boksburg
Tel: (011) 397 5160

Tile Africa
108 AG De Witt Drive
Germiston
Tel: (011) 455 2607

Tile Art
3 Wegner Road
Ottery 7800
Tel: (021) 73 1905

The Tile Doctor
PO Box 5052
Cape Town 8000
Tel: (021) 535 2220

Tile Grip (TVL) (Pty) Ltd
119 Watt Place
Kya Sands, Randburg
Tel: (011) 708 2829

Union Tiles
Cnr. North Reef and Main Road
Bedfordview East
Tel: (011) 455 4220

NEW ZEALAND

Gisborne Tile Warehouse
Cnr. Roebuck and Leith Streets
Gisborne

Midas Design Centre
404 Beach Road
Mairangi Bay

Miles of Tiles Christchurch
175 Ferry Road
Christchurch

New Plymouth Tile Warehouse
116-122 Gill Street
New Plymouth

Placemakers Wanganui
59a Wilson Street
Wanganui

Rotorua Tile Warehouse
262 Te Ngae Road
Rotorua

Southern Tile Warehouse
102 Montreal Street
Christchurch

Takanini Tile Warehouse
180 Great South Road
Takanini

Tauranga Tile Warehouse
18 Marsh Street
Tauranga

Tile Warehouse
286 Church Street
Penrose

Tile Warehouse
120 Wairau Road
Glenfield

Tile Warehouse
225 Thorndon Quay
Wellington

Authors' acknowledgments

Paul and Paul would like to thank everyone at Conran Octopus, Joe Joyce at The Studio and Christine Brickman at Wallis and all our families.